DATE DUE

MAR 28	APR 19	SEP 28
FEB 19 OCT 08		OCT 03
FEB 11		NOV 28
APR 8	APR 19	
FEB 27		
FEB 19	DEC 19	SEP 17 MAY 15
JAN 04		OCT 25
FEB 04 OCT 25		
FEB 04	OCT 25	
APR 30		
	OCT 25	

HIGHSMITH 45230

JENKS EAST ELEMENTARY MEDIA D

Lowriders

E.D. Lake

Illustrated with photographs
by Peter Ford

Reading consultant:
John Manning, Professor of Reading
University of Minnesota

Capstone Press
MINNEAPOLIS

Copyright © 1995 Capstone Press. All rights reserved. No part of this book may be reproduced in any form without written permission from the publisher.

Printed in the United States of America.

Capstone Press • 2440 Fernbrook Lane • Minneapolis, MN 55447

Editorial Director   John Coughlan
Managing Editor   John Martin
Copy Editor   Gil Chandler

Library of Congress Cataloging-in-Publication Data

Lake, E.D., 1950-
   Lowriders / E.D. Lake.
     p. cm. --
   Includes bibliographical references and index.
   ISBN 1-56065-217-9
   1. Lowriders--Juvenile literature. 2. Automobiles--Customizing--Juvenile literature. [1. Lowriders. 2 Automobiles--Customizing.] I. Title.
TL255.2.L35   1995
629.222--dc20   94-22829
                                                                      CIP
                                                                        AC

ISBN: 1-56065-217-9

99 98 97 96   8 7 6 5 4 3 2

Table of Contents

Chapter 1 What Lowriding is All About 5

Chapter 2 The Hydraulics 13

Chapter 3 The Wheels 23

Chapter 4 The Paint Job 25

Chapter 5 Inside a Lowrider 31

Chapter 6 Lowrider Bicycles 35

Chapter 7 Making a Personal Statement 39

Glossary 44

To Learn More 46

Some Useful Addresses 46

Index 47

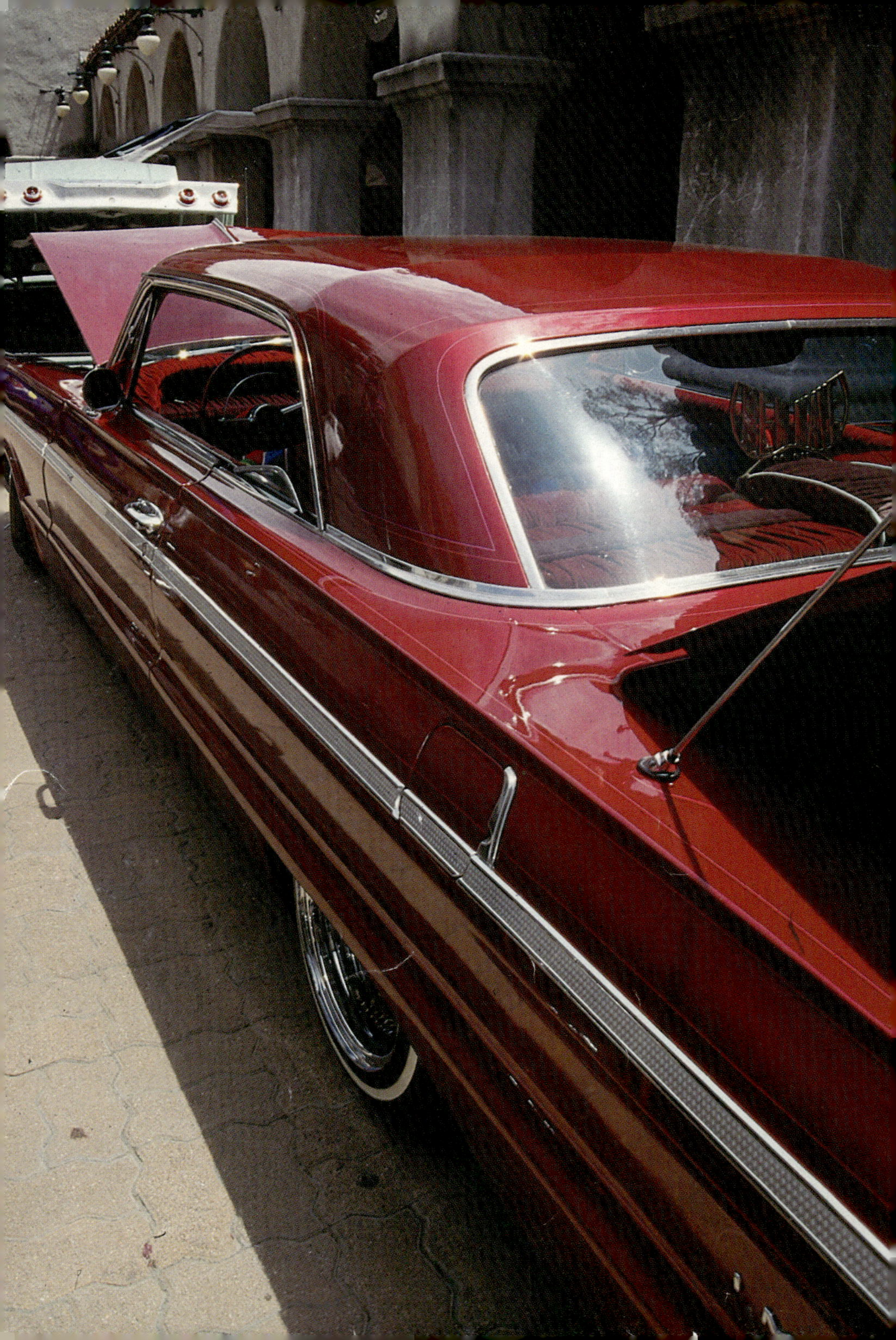

Chapter 1
What Lowriding is All About

After months of saving your money, you buy a 1963 Chevy Impala. You install small wire wheels and a **hydraulic suspension system**.

You paint the outside of the car a deep, shiny red and add gold trim. You **re-upholster** the inside of the car with red-and-gold velvet seat covers.

Your 1963 Chevy Impala sits just inches above the pavement. It's a long, lean lowriding machine.

You're ready to cruise.

Older lowriders have fancy hood ornaments and shiny front grilles.

The Look

Lowriding is not about speed. It's about a look–a low, sleek, and smooth look.

Any vehicle can become a lowrider. People have made lowriders out of automobiles, trucks, vans, and even motorcycles. Young people have even made bicycles into lowriders.

Lowrider owners spend hours changing their vehicles. They pay close attention to details. They put many coats of paint on a car to make it as glossy as possible. Some even cover their car's engine and undercarriage with chrome. Every inch of a lowrider must be clean and shiny.

It's the look, not the machine, that counts.

Where Lowriding Started

Lowriding began back in the 1940s in the *barrios*, or Mexican-American neighborhoods, of southern California. Since then it has spread to other areas of the country and even overseas.

Some of the newest and most enthusiastic lowrider fans are Japanese. One recent lowrider show in Tokyo, Japan, attracted more than 5,000 people.

This 1940s model—a classic "lead slead"—dates to the beginnings of lowriding.

Most lowriders, however, still cruise the **Chicano** communities of the southwestern United States, from San Antonio, Texas, to San José, California. In those cities, lowriders are called by their Spanish name, *carros bajos*.

"You'll never be able to beat Chicanos at lowriding," says Alberto Lopez, the publisher of *Lowrider* magazine. "We have the best cars now and we'll always have the best cars. The creativity, the taste, the heart–we have it all."

"Lead Sleds"

Some of the earliest lowriders were made from "lead sleds," the heavy, bulky American cars popular in the 1930s, 1940s, and 1950s. Two classic lead sleds are the 1936 Ford and the 1952 Mercury.

These cars came out of the factory already looking low and elegant. Many had fender **skirts**–extra steel siding that covered part of their rear wheels. These skirts added to the smooth, sleek appearance of the cars.

Many lead-sled owners enjoy fixing up their old cars.

Other owners create completely new vehicles with their old lead sleds. They give their cars special paint jobs and fancy interiors. They add air conditioning, expensive sound systems, and other features.

These changes turn the lead sled into a new kind of classic–a classic lowrider.

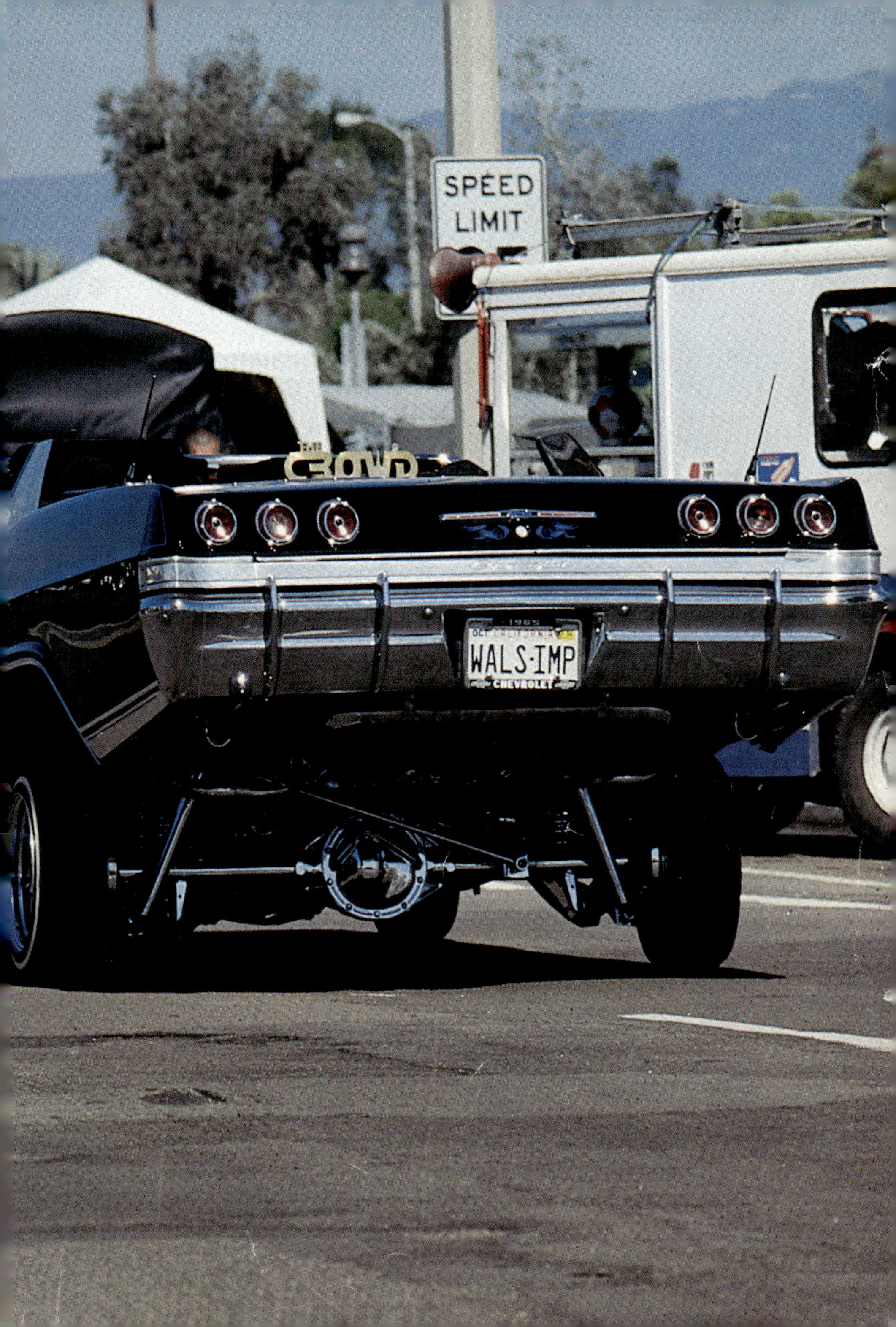
SPEED
LIMIT
WALS-IMP
CHEVROLET

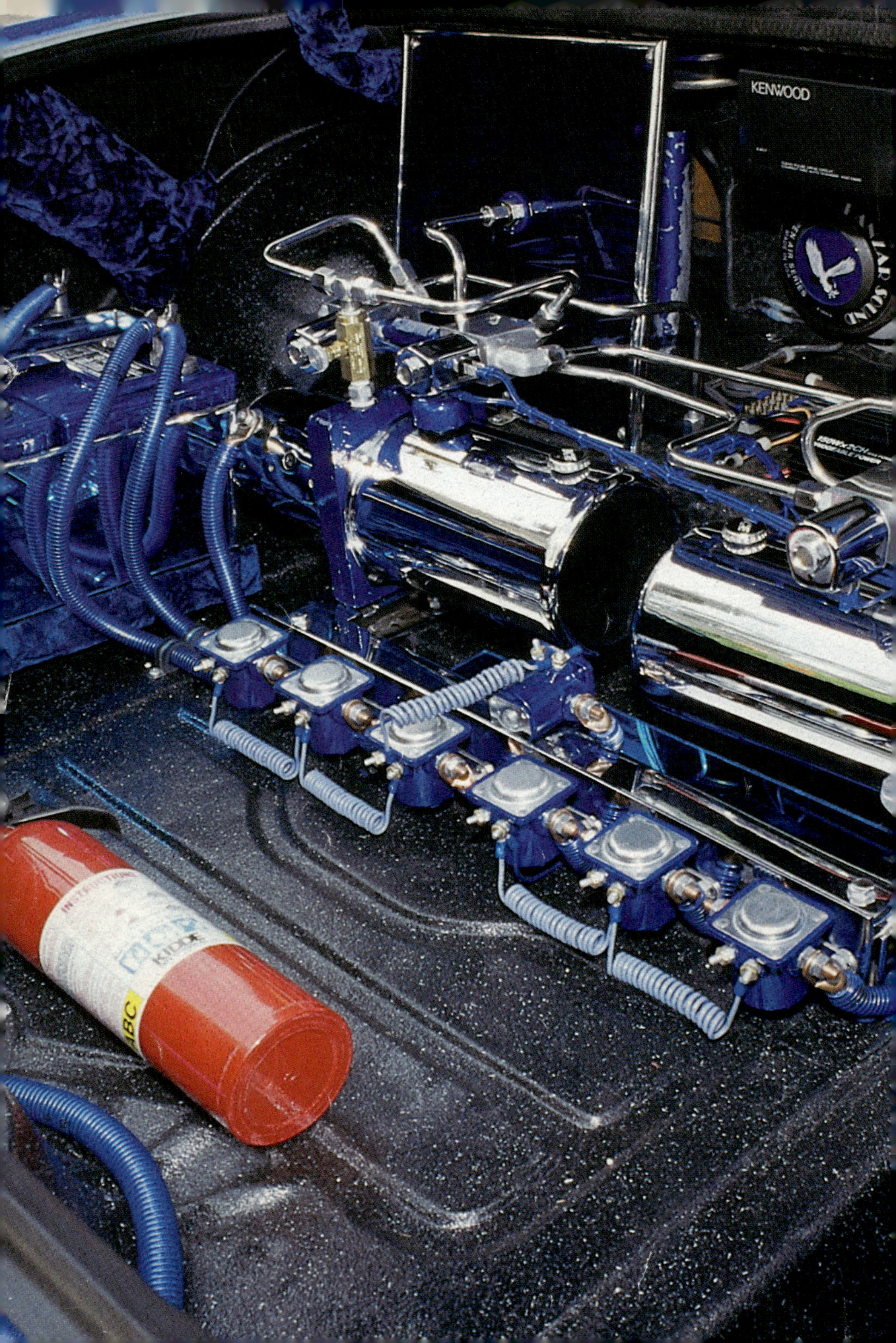
KENWOOD
KIDDE
ABC

Chapter 2
The Hydraulics

Back in the 1940s, people gave their lowriders that down-to-the-ground look by filling their car trunks with bags of cement. Lowrider fans now get the same effect with special hydraulic suspension systems.

These devices can lift a car high above its wheels to clear a bump or a curb. For slow cruising, hydraulics can drop the car to ride only an inch or two above the road.

How Hydraulic Suspension Works

The average car has coil springs on all four wheels. The springs soften the ride over bumps and ruts in the road. **Shock absorbers** steady the car after a bump. Without this **suspension** system, the car would be unsteady and dangerous.

Lowrider owners remove the springs and front shock absorbers from their cars. Then they install a special hydraulic system. A typical lowrider system has four fluid-filled **cylinders**. Two cylinders replace the front

Hydraulic pumps in the trunk allow the lowrider driver to raise and lower the car.

After adding these parts to the lowrider, the driver can hop and bounce.

shocks, while the other two are welded to the car's rear **axle**.

The cylinders are connected to a hydraulic pump, which is usually placed in the trunk of the car. Four to eight twelve-volt batteries power the pump. (Many lowrider competitors use high-voltage, industrial-sized batteries.)

Hydraulics allow the driver to perform all kinds of maneuvers in a lowrider.

When the driver wants the car to rise, he or she uses one or more **toggle switches** to run the pump. The pump pushes fluid into the cylinders, which then lift the car's body. To lower the car, the driver uses the pump to drain fluid out of the cylinders.

Other Cars with Hydraulics

Lowriders were not the first cars to have hydraulic suspension systems. Citroën, a French automobile company, started using hydraulics many years ago. The Citroën pump automatically lifts and lowers the car as it drives along. It keeps the car level, no matter how bumpy the road.

Some racing cars have computerized hydraulic suspension. The system adjusts the cars to changing road surfaces.

Hops

At lowrider exhibitions, owners show off their hydraulic systems in competitions. The winner of a "hop" is the car or truck whose front wheels bounce farthest off the ground.

A skilled driver can really hug the street with a well-equipped lowrider.

An average lowrider can bounce about 15 to 20 inches (38 to 50 centimeters) into the air. The world-record hop for a lowrider car is 64 inches (163 centimeters). The world record hop for a truck is 72 inches (183 centimeters).

Dancing

Another type of hydraulic competition, called "dancing," is done to loud, rocking

18

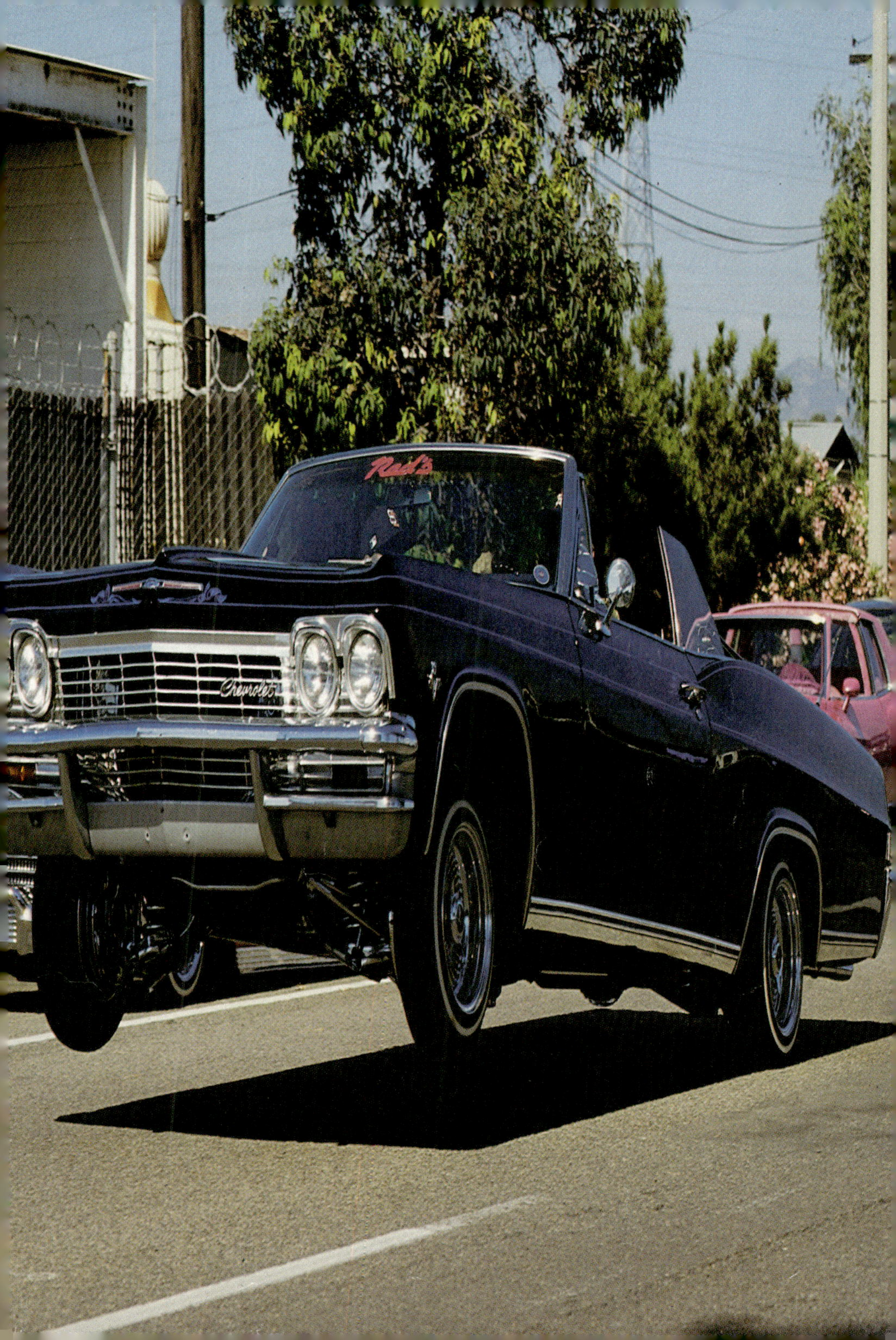
Ned's
Chevrolet

20

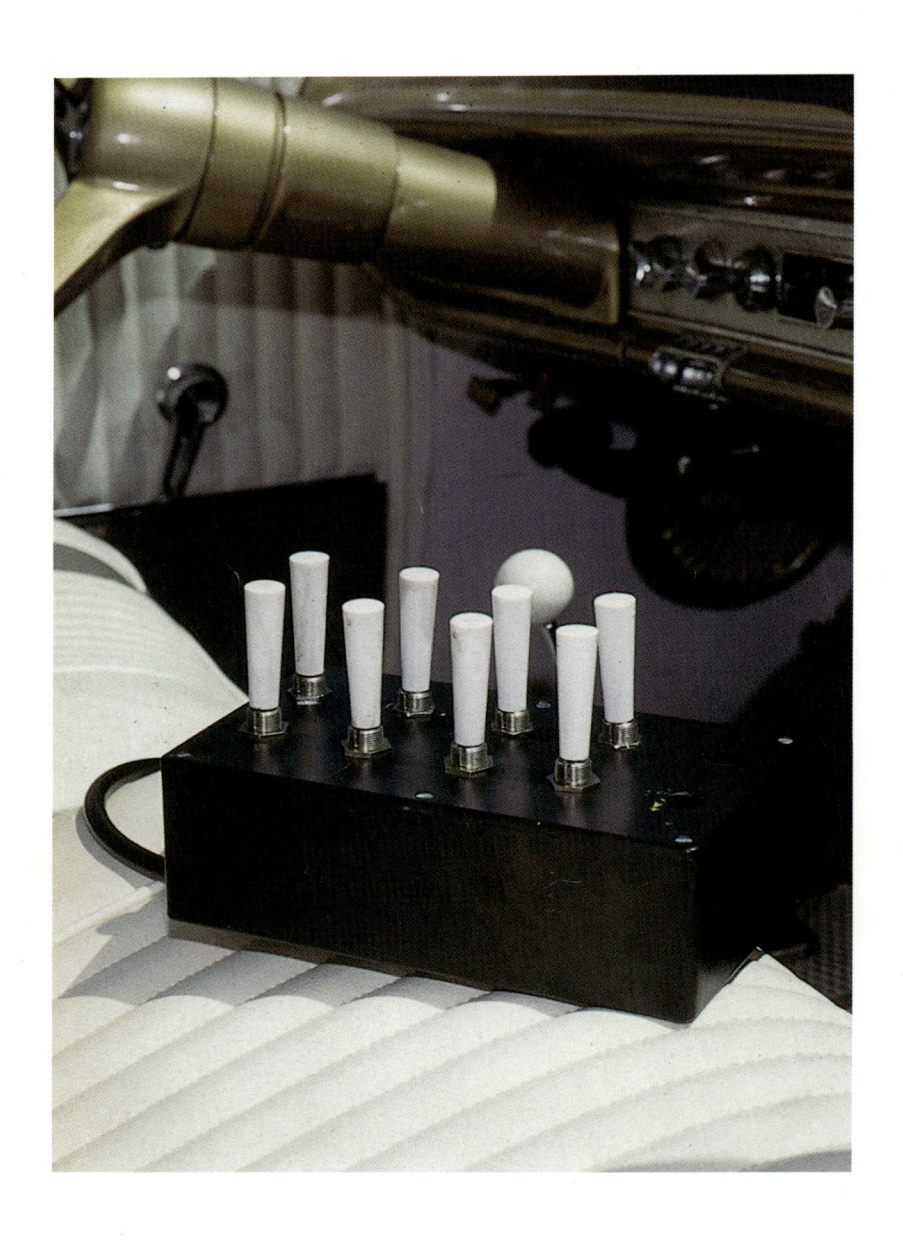

music. The cars jump, lurch, and sway, sometimes turning in 360-degree circles. Contestants win points for putting on the most exciting show.

Bed Dancing

In "bed dancing" contests, lowriding truck owners make their truck beds rise and dance. Some beds open and release dozens of hidden helium balloons into the air.

To get a vehicle jumping, the driver carefully works the hydraulic switches. A lowrider can have as many as 24 toggle switches that send the car hopping up and down.

Some owners like to stay in their cars while their vehicles dance. It can be a wild ride. Others stand outside the car. They work the pumps with a remote-control box connected to the car by heavy cables.

"You can't get any bigger thrill than working that switch," says one lowrider fan.

Working the switches from the front seat can send the car dancing in all directions.

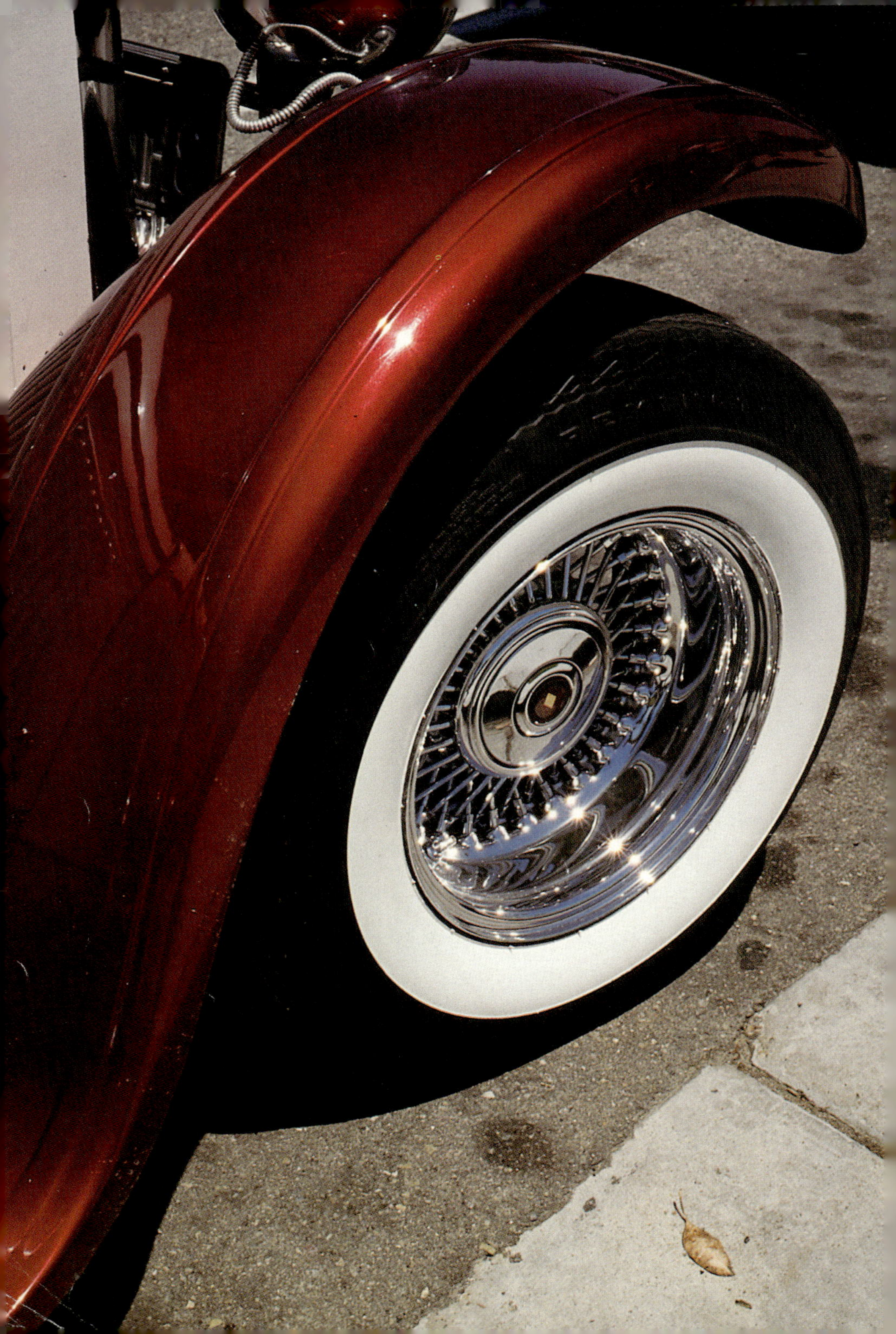

Chapter 3
The Wheels

Lowriders have smaller-than-normal wheels that keep the car close to the ground.

Wire Wheels

Many owners prefer wire wheels with straight spokes. These wheels are light and strong, and they look good.

It's hard for small wheels to carry the weight of a big car. That's one reason owners cruise rather than speed in their lowriders. When you drive fast in a lowrider, you risk having a flat tire, and maybe an accident.

Most lowrider owners, of course, like to go slowly anyway. They want everybody to see and admire their vehicles.

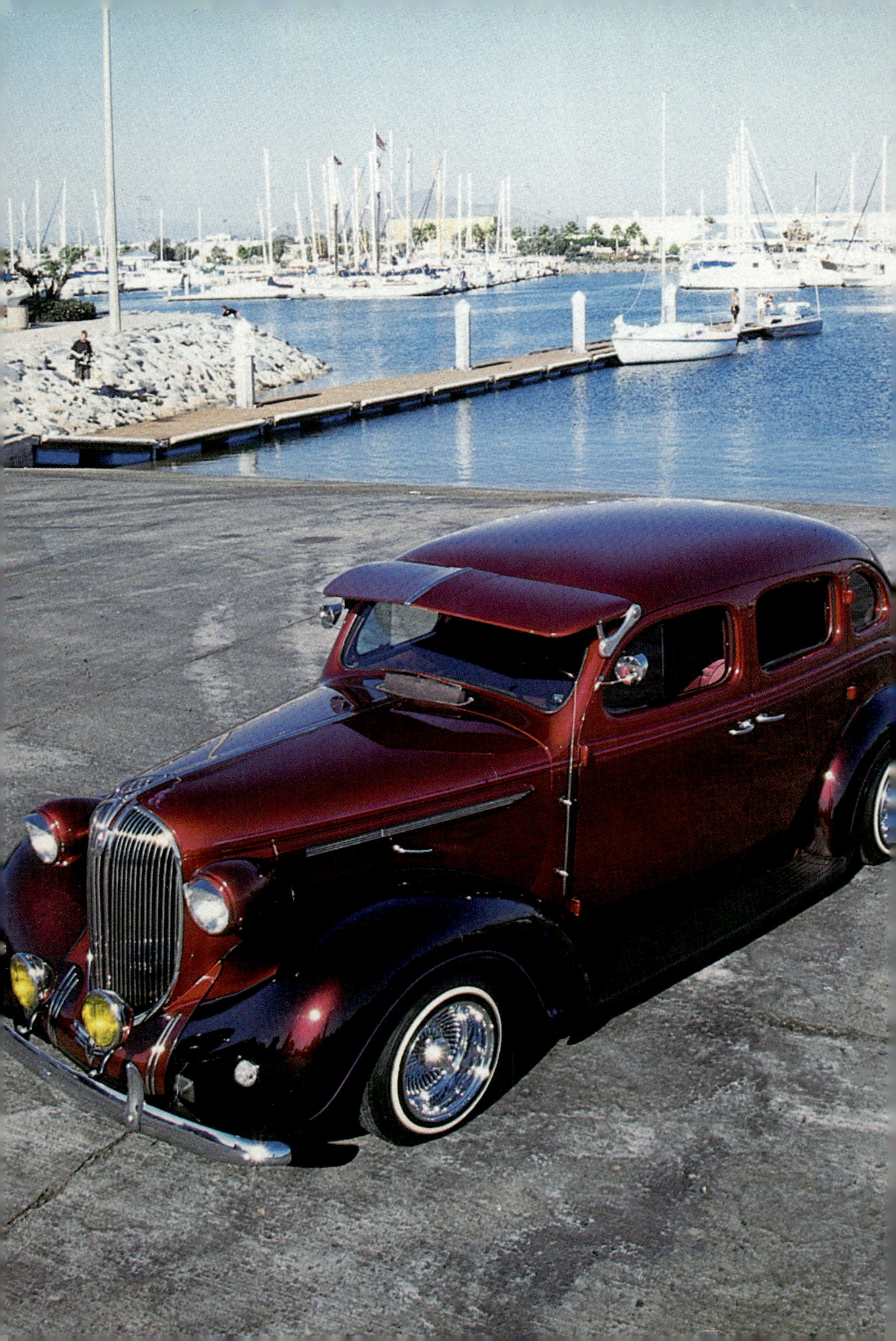

Chapter 4
The Paint Job

Lowriders have to look good. Owners spend a lot of time and money on their car's paint job. They like shiny, "candy" colors–bright yellow, deep red, or rich purple, for example. Some paints have tiny metal flakes in them for a glittery look.

To get the shine they want, owners spray many coats of paint onto the car. Then they cover the paint with layers of see-through **lacquer**. The lacquer gives the paint even more shine and depth.

Murals

Some people paint fade-away stripes, flames, or other patterns onto their lowriders. Others paint scenes called **murals** on the trunks, hoods, or sides of their lowriders. The murals most often depict Mexican folklore.

Undercarriage

Even the **undercarriage** may have a colorful mural. To display their artwork at shows, owners set the vehicles on raised platforms with mirrors.

Under the hood, some lowrider engines are decorated in the same color as the exterior. Designs or murals also dress up the engine, and chrome gleams from every nut, bolt, and steel plate.

Radicals

Gold plating covers the engines and undercarriages of especially fancy lowriders called **radicals**. These vehicles have cost their

The murals on lowriders often depict Mexican folklore.

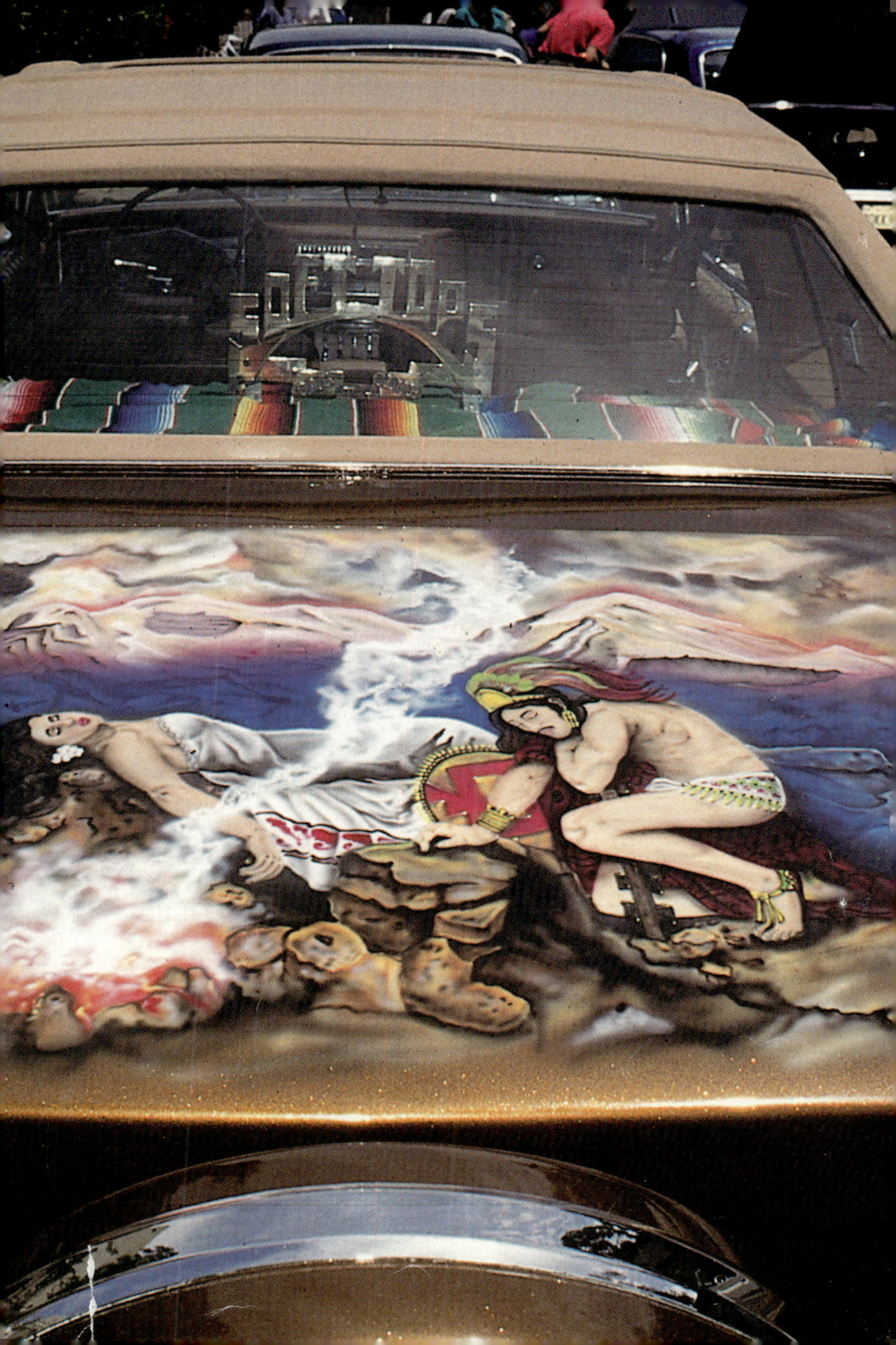

owners thousands of dollars to build and decorate. For this reason, radical owners seldom drive their cars. They transport them to lowrider contests in crates.

Traveling Art

Painting murals on lowriding cars is part of a long tradition that began in Central and South America. For decades, artists in these regions have decorated buses and trucks with paintings. They often paint the entire side of a vehicle. The Mexican culture is the favorite subject among these artists.

Bus painters consider the rear emergency door the best spot for a mural. People following the bus have time to view the paintings there. Artists put their best work on the rear door, and they proudly sign their paintings.

The Mexican hero Zapata is the subject of this lowrider mural.

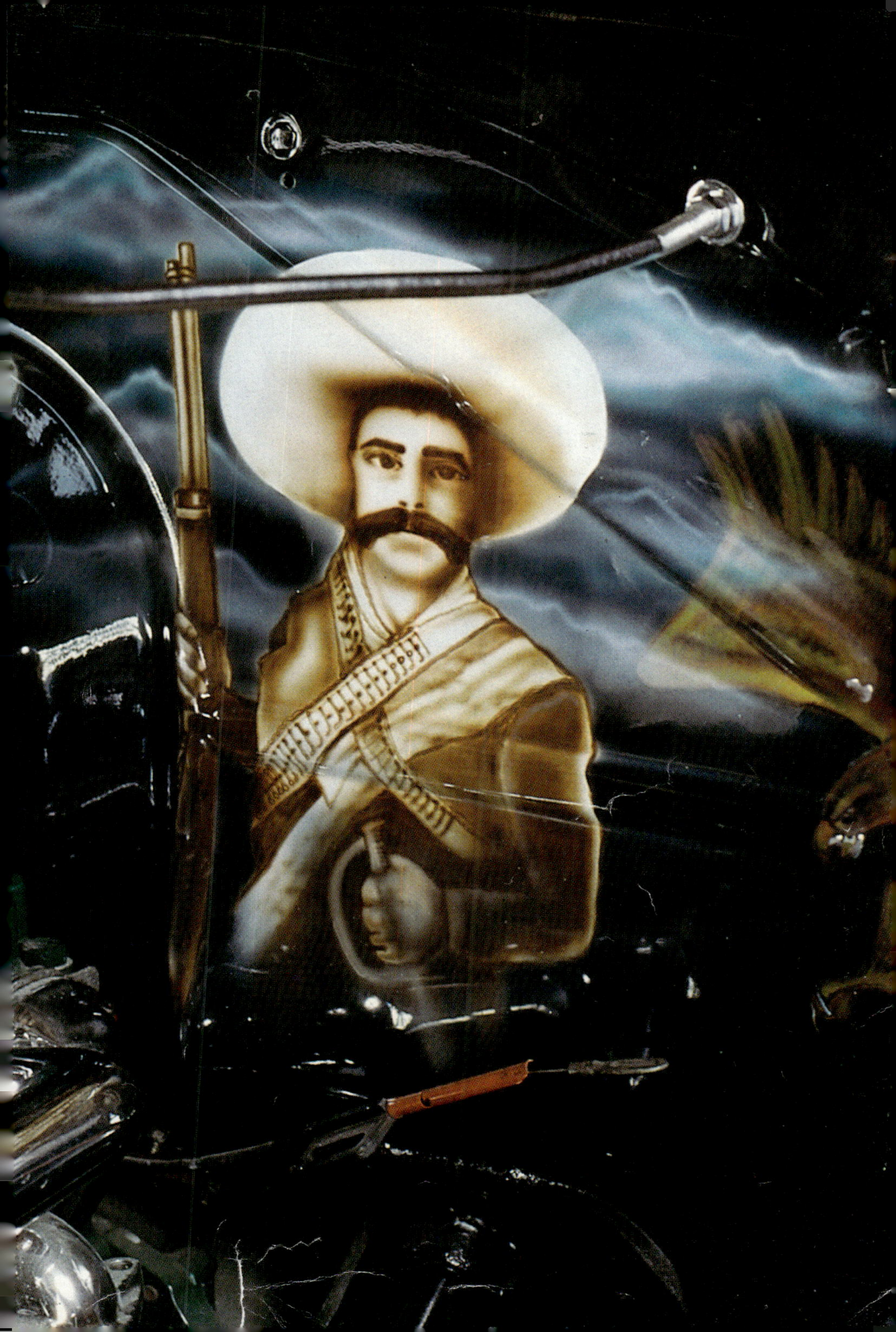

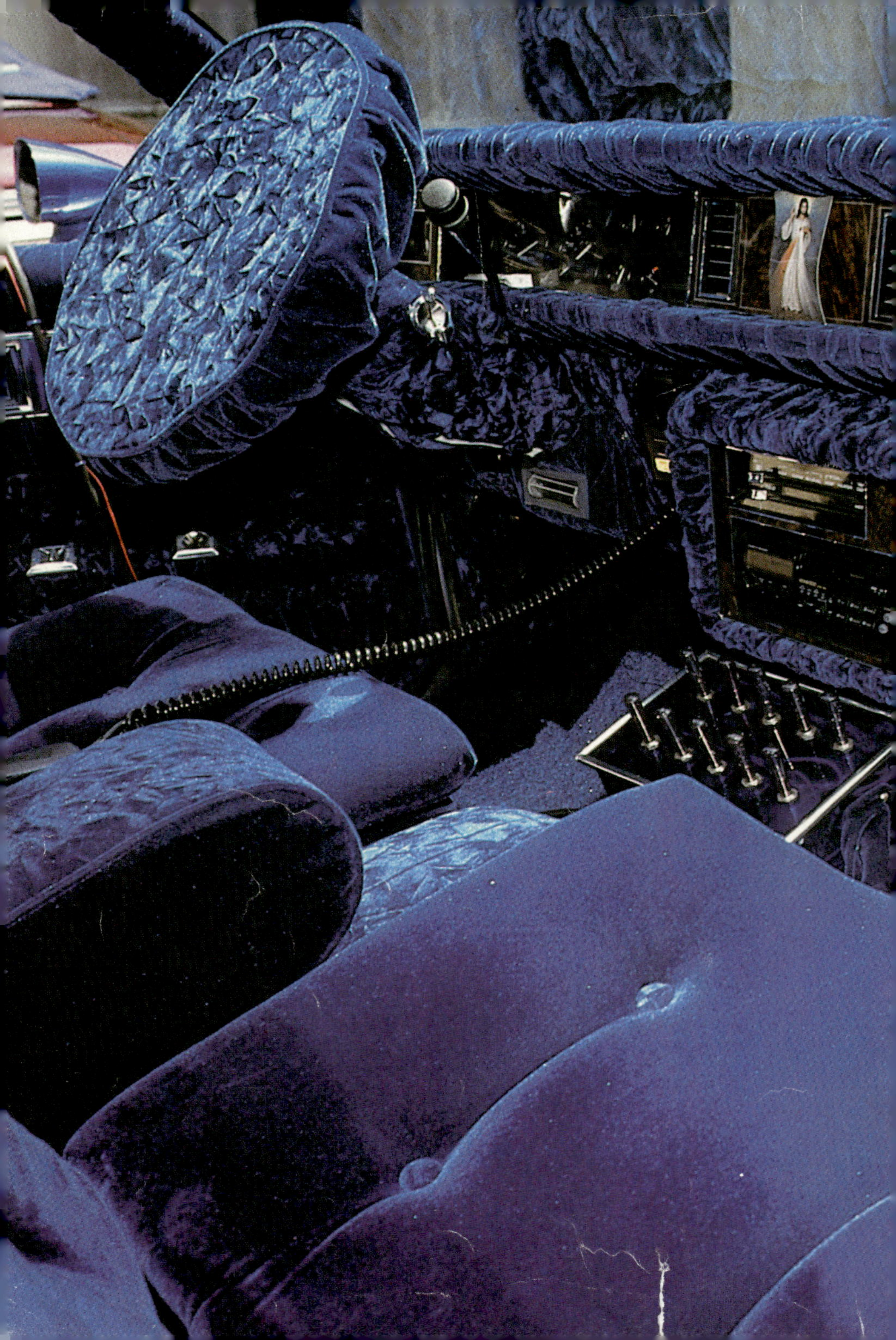

Chapter 5
Inside a Lowrider

Lowriders have plush interiors to match their glossy exteriors. Owners often change the interior of the car or truck completely. They put velvet or **velour** upholstery on the seats, steering wheel, dashboard, door panels, and floors. Soft materials line the inside of the trunk and the head of the engine.

Owners add plenty of extras to make the interior even fancier. Popular extras include gold-plated steering columns, a steering wheel of welded chain links, and swivel seats. Some owners even put fountains and fish tanks in the back seats!

The Sound System

A very important lowrider item is the sound system. Expensive stereo cassette or compact disc players sit in the dashboard mounts. There has to be plenty of space in the car for the loudspeakers. Some vehicles have as many as 20. Most lowriders have **woofers** and **tweeters**, two different types of loudspeakers. The woofers send out low musical tones; the tweeters send out the high tones. Together, they create a broad, clear, thunderous sound.

Neon Tubing

Some lowrider owners install neon tubing on the undercarriage of their vehicles. Neon gives a car or truck an exciting electric glow. For a really special effect, the neon is hooked up to the sound system. The light then pulses in time to the music.

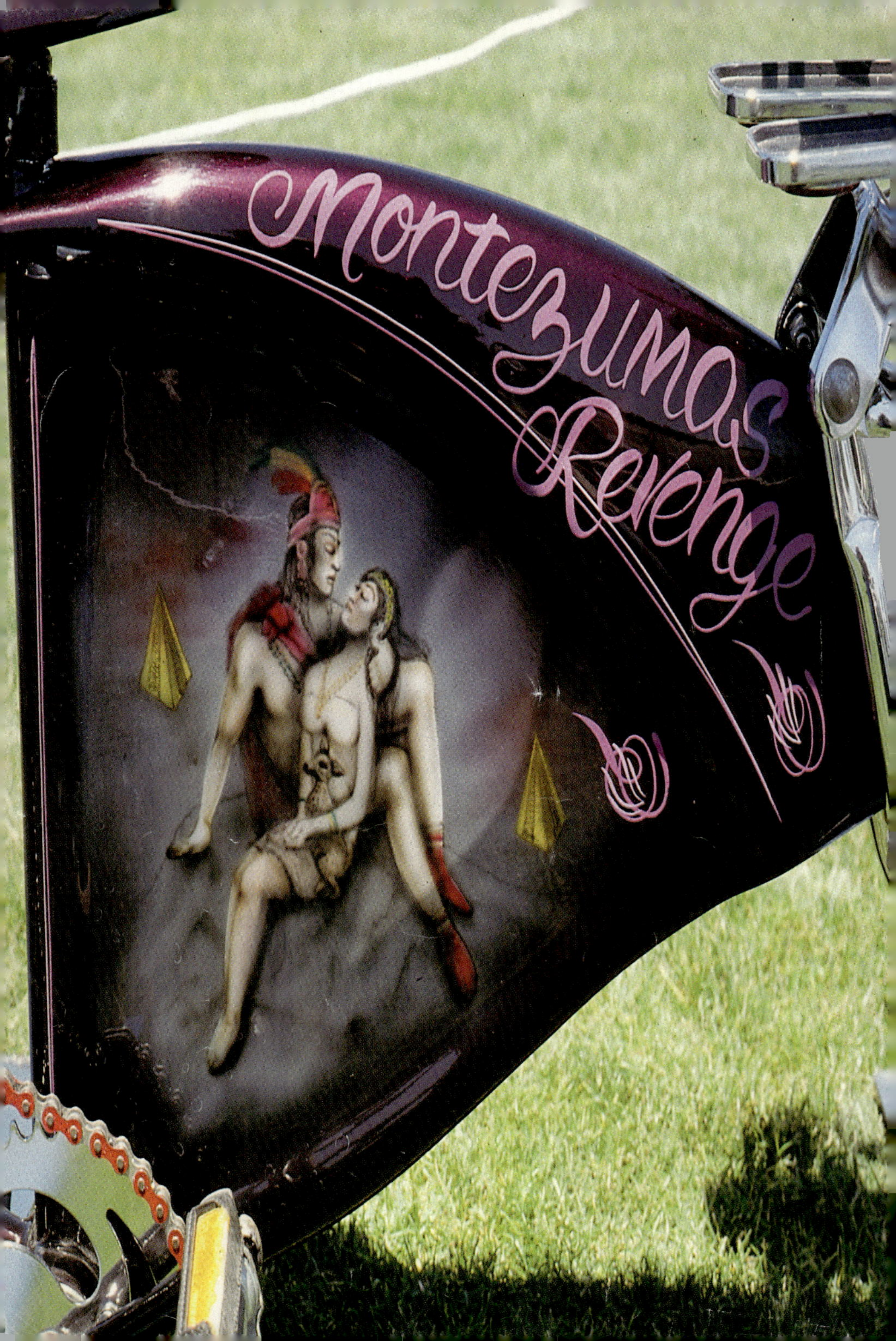
Montezumas
Revenge

Chapter 6
Lowrider Bicycles

Building a lowrider bicycle requires some time, some money, and a lot of imagination. Just look at what Juan Martinez did with an old Schwinn bicycle.

Juan bought the bike from a friend for five dollars. With help from his dad, he reshaped the frame to make it look more like a motorcycle. He even added a motorcycle-like saddle with a colorful Mexican **serape** cover.

The bike has a chain with red links, ape-hanger handlebars, two mirrors, a loud stereo and a television set.

Juan painted the bike a deep **acrylic** purple. A friend of his dad painted a mural on it.

Juan calls his lowrider bike *Montezuma's Revenge*. Montezuma was an **Aztec** leader.

The Aztecs were the ancient Indian people of Mexico. It's a great name for a truly amazing lowriding creation.

37

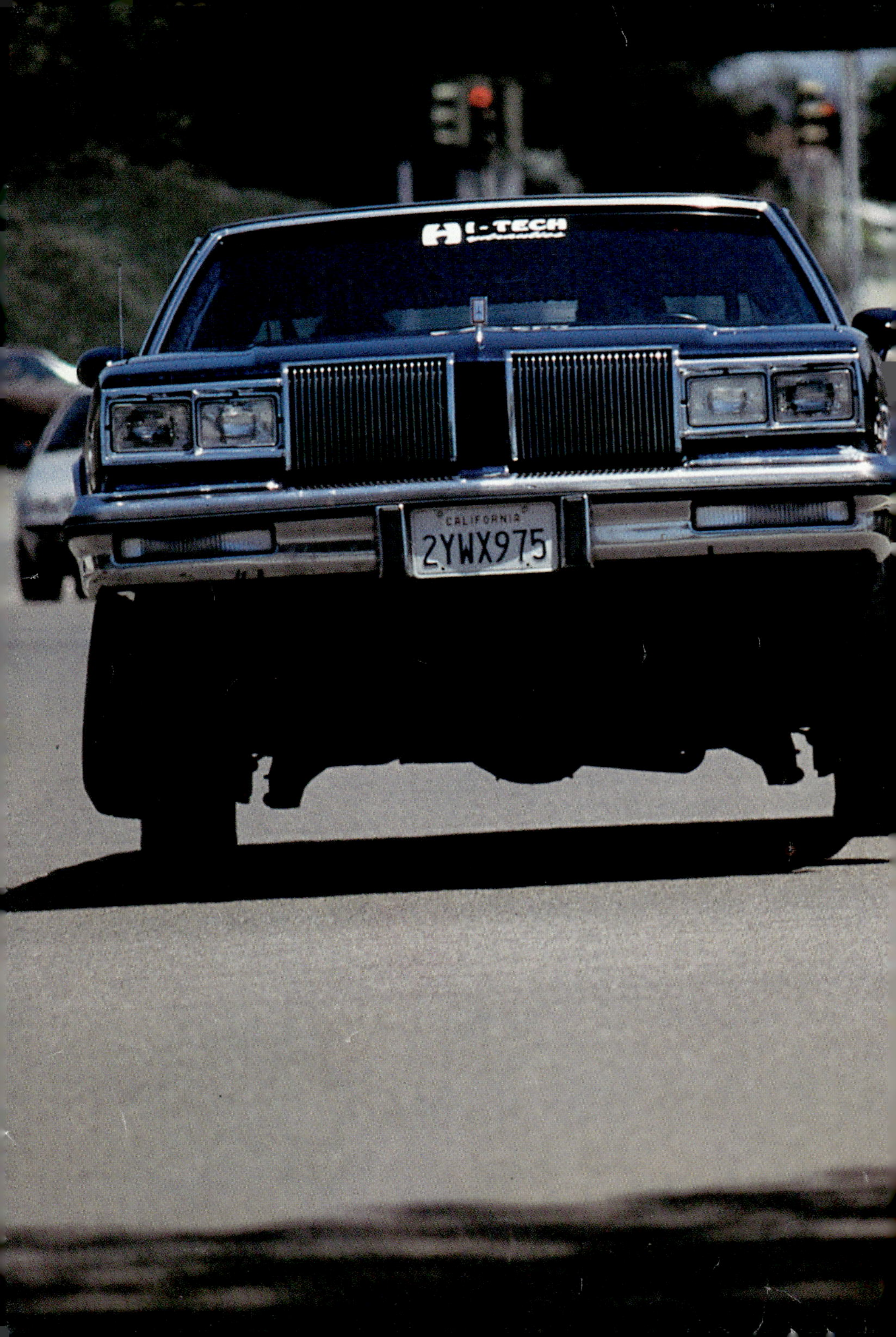
CALIFORNIA
2YWX975

Chapter 7

Making a Personal Statement

W hy do people enjoy lowriding?
To begin with, they like the look. "When I got involved with cars, it was the long, lean, low look that attracted me," says one lowriding fan. "It was the way the cars looked when they were cruising. They weren't just rolling by. They were hugging the earth."

It's not just the look that attracts thousands of people to lowriding. Fans also like the idea of expressing themselves with their vehicles.

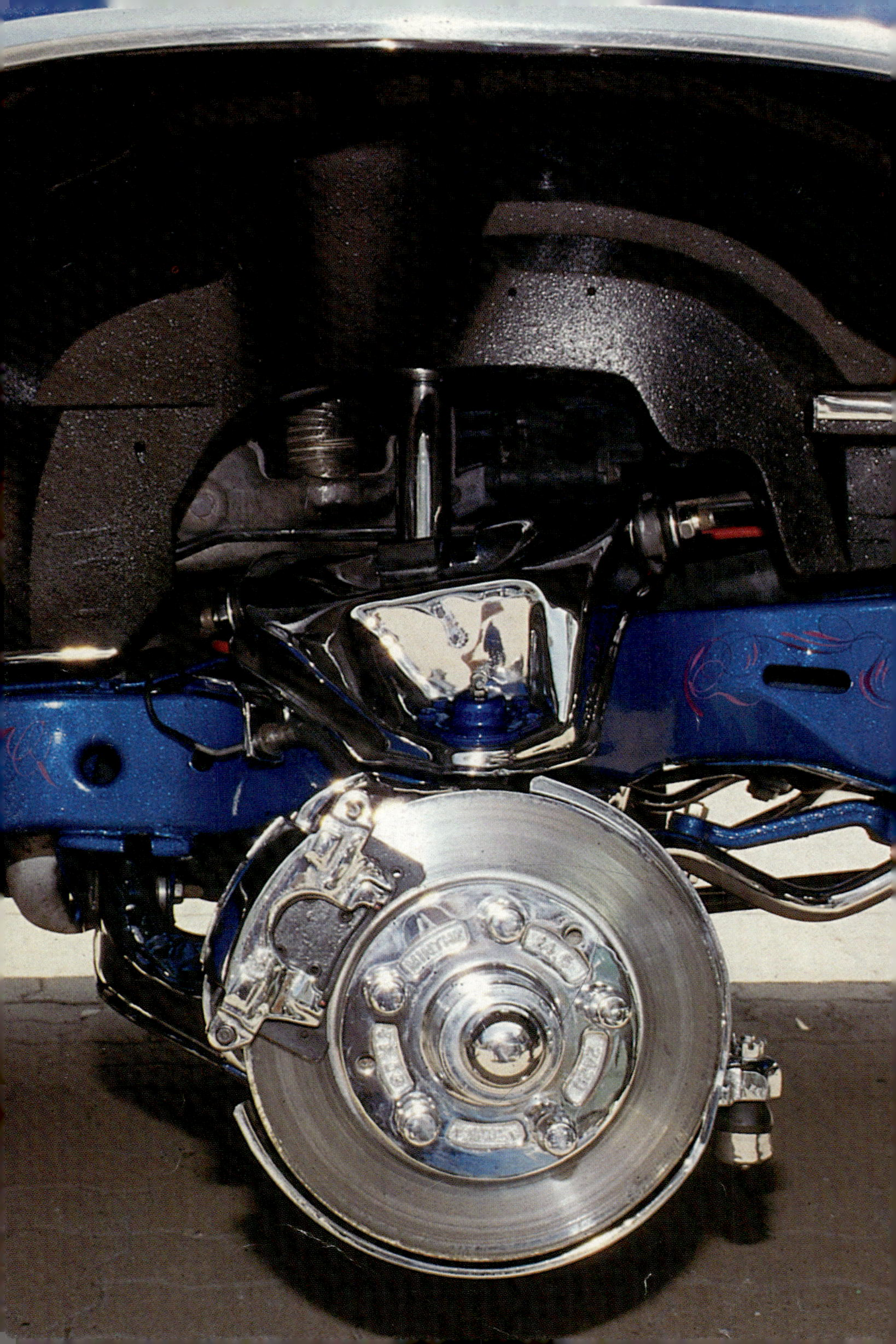

"It's a way of modifying your vehicle so it stands out from the crowd," explains a long-time lowriding enthusiast. "Each car has its own personality."

Each car also has a great deal of hard work and creative energy behind it. Great pride in their Chicano culture influences the many

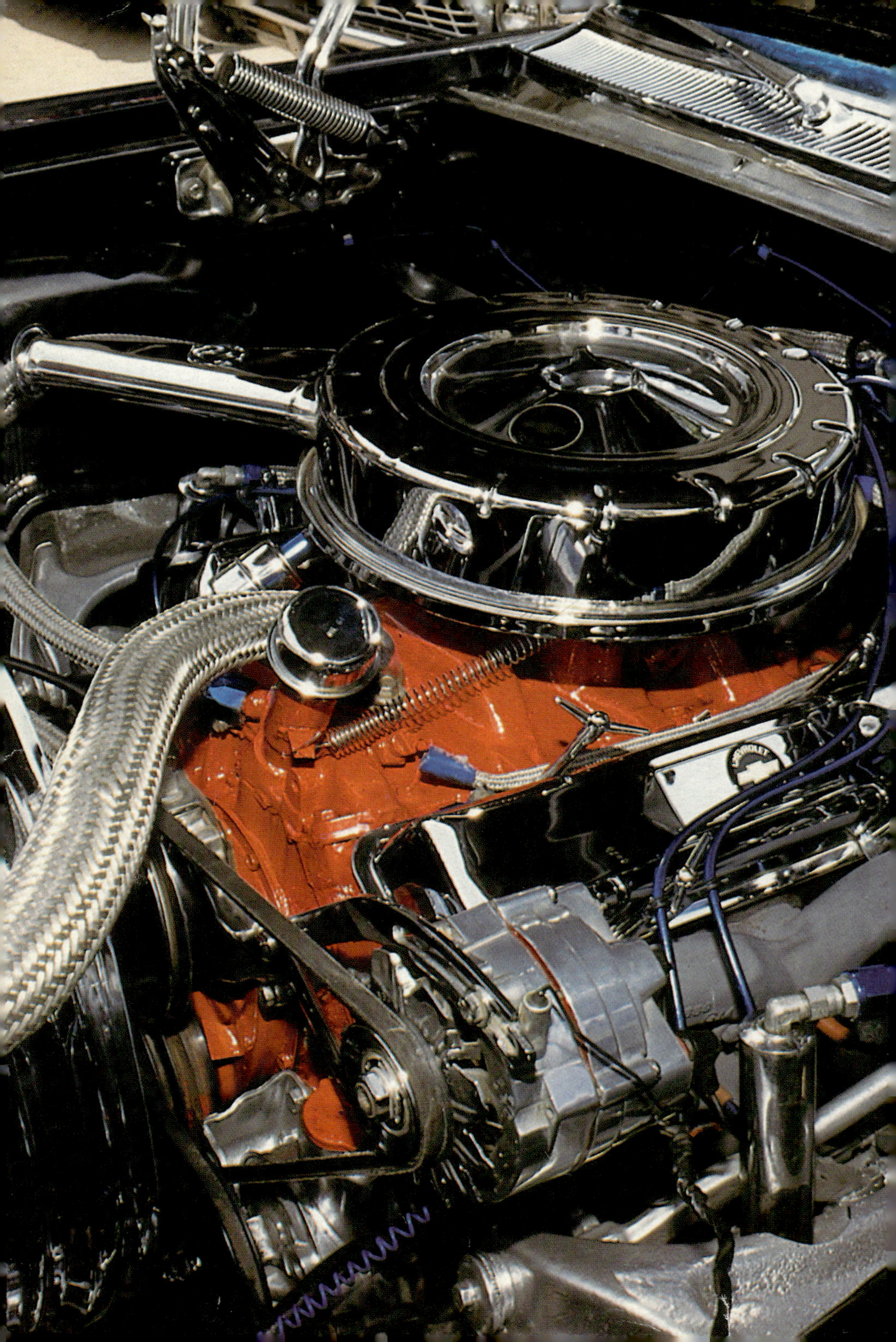

Mexican-American lowrider owners. To many, lowriders are not just cars. They are a way of life.

Lowriders are truly works of art, from their candy-colored paint jobs to their chrome-plated engines. But unlike other works of art, these masterpieces can cruise.

Glossary

acrylic–a tough, glossy paint that comes in bright colors

axle–the metal rod on which the wheel of a car or truck spins

Aztec–the name for the ancient Indian people of Mexico

barrios–areas of a city or town where many of the people come from Latin America and speak Spanish

Chicano–a person of Mexican-American descent

cylinders–objects shaped like long, narrow tubes

hydraulic suspension system–a suspension system on a car or truck that uses fluid-filled cylinders rather than coil springs

lacquer–a clear varnish

mural–a painting on a wall or other permanent surface

radicals–the fanciest class of lowrider vehicles

re-upholster–to re-cover a seat or surface with new fabric

serape–a colorful Mexican shawl worn over the shoulders

skirts–pieces of steel which cover part of the rear wheels

shock absorbers–devices that stop a vehicle's springs from continuing to bounce after hitting a bump

suspension–the springs and shock absorbers on the wheels of a car or truck; they make the ride smoother and safer

tweeters–the loudspeakers that pick up and reproduce high-pitched sounds

toggle switch–a switch that works a hydraulic pump, lowering or raising the car

undercarriage–the supporting framework of a car or truck

velour–a fabric that feels and looks much like velvet

woofers–the loudspeakers that pick up and reproduce low-pitched sounds

To Learn More

Barrett, Norman S. *Custom Cars.* New York: Franklin Watts, 1987.

Murphy, Jim. *Custom Car: A Nuts and Bolts Guide to Building One.* New York: Clarion Books, 1989.

Ready, Kirk L. *Custom Cars.* Minneapolis: Lerner Publications, 1982

You can read articles about lowriders in two magazines: *Lowrider* and *Lowrider Bicycle.*

Some Useful Addresses

Lowrider and **Lowrider Bicycle** magazines
Park Avenue Publishing, Inc.
P.O. Box 648
Walnut, CA 91788-0648

Plaza de la Raza
3540 N. Mission Road
Los Angeles, CA 90031

Index

axles, 15
Aztecs, 36

barrios, 7
batteries, 15
bicycles, 7, 35-36
buses, 28

California, 7
Central America, 28
Chevy Impala, 5
Chicanos, 9, 41
Citroën, 17
coil springs, 13-14

dancing, 18, 21

engines, 7, 26, 31, 43

Ford, 10

grilles, 10

hops, 17-18
hydraulic pumps, 15-17
hydraulic suspension, 5, 13-17

interiors, 31

lacquer, 25
lead sleds, 10
Lopez, Alberto, 9
Lowrider magazine, 9

Martinez, Juan, 35-36
Mercury, 10
Mexico, 26, 28, 37
motorcycles, 7
murals, 26, 28

neon, 33
paint, 5, 7, 10, 25-26, 36, 43

radicals, 26, 28

San Antonio, Texas, 8
San Jose, California, 8
Schwinn, 41
seats, 5, 31
shock absorbers, 14-15
skirts, 10
sound systems, 10, 32-33, 35
South America, 28
suspension, 14

tailfins, 10

toggle switches, 16, 21
Tokyo, Japan, 7
trim, 5
trucks, 7

undercarriages, 7, 26, 33
upholstery, 31

vans, 7
velour, 31
velvet, 5, 31

wheels, 17, 23